Coaching youth soccer in England:

An investigation into coaching behaviour, session content and coach education within football.

By

Dave Earnden

Dave Earnden
2015

First Printing: 2015

ISBN 978-1-326-49063-8

Dave Earnden
Spires Gardens
Warrington, Cheshire. WA2 8WB

www.daveearndencoaching.com & www.planmype.com

Coaching youth soccer in England:
An investigation into coaching behaviour, session content and coach education within football.

Dedication

My wife, **Kim**, for putting up with me, supporting me, pushing me and calming me throughout my final year – I love you.

My son, **Cody**, who will always be my inspiration in everything – I love you.

My **Mum and Dad,** for all of their unconditional love and support throughout the last five years, I could not have done this without you – I love you.

My **Grandparents,** for giving me their unconditional support & love throughout my time at University – I love you.

Contents

Abstract

Through the analysis of systematic observation of youth football coaches, the purpose of this study was to determine if there were any relationships between coaches behaviour, the experience, education, football qualifications gained and the content which is being delivered in training sessions. The Arizona State University Observation Instrument and an adapted version of System for Observing Fitness Instruction Time (SOFIT) namely (SOCAB) System for Observing practice Content And coach Behaviour was used to compile data on youth football coaches during a three month period of one football season.

Previous research on coaching expertise has used a combination of several criteria to determine the appropriate coaches for study Cote, Salmela and Russell (1995); these criteria included the number of years of coaching experience and officially recognized qualifications and skills, Cote *et al* (1995). Following on from cote *et al* (1995) research criterion, the coaches were profiled by using the following categories: coaching experience, playing experience, English FA coaching qualifications, further education and age group which they coached.

This study is in agreement to that of previous studies (Tharp and Gallimore 1976, Langsdorf 1979, Dodds and Rife 1981, and Lacy and Darst 1985), which found that the use of instruction was the most commonly used behaviour by the coaches with general instruction scoring (m = 59.50%). Out of the three types of instruction, concurrent instruction (m = 19.31%) scored highest with post instruction (m = 8.95%) scoring the least. However, a Pearson correlation test was performed and showed that there was no positive correlation between concurrent instruction and the use of praise (r = 7.73, n = 14, p> .0005). Independent T-tests identified that coaches with a FA Level 2 certificate (mean = 15.43 ± 4.91) do in fact use silence more than those with a FA Level 1 certificate (6.26 ± 3.84). However, when testing the use of silence by coaching experience it was coaches with 5 – 7 years coaching experience (mean = 18.88 ± 0.98) which scored higher than coaches with 7 years or above experience (mean = 6.63 ± 4.36).

Whilst instruction remained the single highest scoring behaviour category, it was not possible to establish exactly what was being said during this time, therefore further testing and observational methods would be necessary to establish exactly what was being said during this time. More, McGarry, Partridge and Franks (1996) used the Coach Analysis Instrument (CAI) which is an instrument used to systematically examine the effectiveness of verbal coaching behaviour and to record verbal content from a coach. By introducing this additional system, a more accurate data could be recorded.

This study has not only augmented previous studies and theories, it has also contradicted them. It indicates just how complex coaching behaviour can be when viewing it in a behavioural context surrounding the coaching process. Whilst this study has highlighted the common behaviours used by youth football coaches during a practice session and illustrated what factors may have affected these behaviours, there are still many areas within the coaching environment and the coaching process which need to be explored in more depth. However, it is hoped that this study can be used as a foundation on which to build upon in respect to future studies surrounding youth football coaching ensuring that an even more critical understanding of coach behaviour, coach education and the coaching process can be achieved.

Tables & Figures

Tables

Figures

Introduction

Through the analysis of systematic observation of youth football coaches, the purpose of this study was to determine if there were any relationships between coaches behaviour, the experience, education, football qualifications gained and the content which is being delivered in training sessions. The Arizona State University Observation Instrument and an adapted version of System for Observing Fitness Instruction Time (SOFIT) namely (SOCAB) System for Observing practice Content And coach Behaviour was used to compile data on youth football coaches during a three month period of one football season. Potrac, Jones and Cushion (2007) explain that the ASUOI instrument was designed to collect information on the behaviours of coaches in the practice environment using a ten category system originally developed and designed by Tharp and Gallimore (1976) for systematically observing coach behaviour within a coaching setting. McKenzie, Sallis and Nadar (1991) describe SOFIT as a direct observation instrument designed to assess variables associated with students' activity levels. McKenzie *et al* (1991) continue to explain that SOFIT involves the systematic observation of physical education classes while simultaneously recording student physical activity levels, curriculum context variables, and teacher behaviour. However, because of the purpose of this study where physical activity levels are not being observed and analysed, the SOFIT instrument had to be adapted.

Sports coaching must be understood as a complex and messy process Cross and Lyle (2000). Cross and Lyle (2000) continue and state that the coach, the relationship between athlete and coach, coaching practice and behaviour, and the training and competition elements, are all part of the coaching process. Furthermore, research over the last decade has demonstrated that it is experience and the observation of other coaches that remain the primary sources of knowledge for coaches, yet despite this, coach education and continuing professional development fail to draw effectively on this experience (Gould, Gianinni, Krane and Hodge 1990, Salmela 1996, Cushion 2001, Gilbert and Trudel 2001, and Cushion, Armour and Jones 2003). Furthermore, Gould *et al* (1990), Salmela *et al* (1994) and Cushion *et al* (2003), also explain that observation of other coaches, experience and qualifications play a role in coaching behaviour. However, Gilbert, Cote and Mallet (2006) and Werthner and Trudel (2006) explain that although there are many different behaviours used during a coaching session, other factors outside of the coaching process and educational programs can influence these behaviours. Rodgers, Reade and Hall (2007) explain that age and sex of the coach, the coach's years of experience, their levels of formal education and coach specific education, as well as their competitive background, for example personal involvement as an athlete, could all be factors why the coach behaves in such a manner. Much research within the coaching environment has stemmed from the desire to further understand what happens in the coaching/learning environment and has generated a considerable amount of analytical data (Potrac, Brewer, Jones, Armour and Hoff 2000). De Marco, Mancini, Wuest and Schempp (1996) explain that the predominant stratagem used for such research has been systematic observation.

Tharp and Gallimore (1976) conducted the first descriptive study of systematic observation on a coach; they intended to provide information on the coaching behaviour of a successful collegiate basketball coach. Systematic observations continued to be the ideal methodology in future studies and were used by Langsdorf (1979), Dodds and Rife (1981), Lacy and Darst (1985) and Claxton (1988) to help further the knowledge and understanding of the coaching environment. Potrac *et al* (2000) explain that the role of systematic observation in providing baseline data of actual coaching behaviours has also been established as a precursor to identify, through the accompanying use of qualitative methodologies, answers relating to a more general understanding of what, to date, has been considered an esoteric coaching process. Therefore, systematic observation also has a function as a procedural step in answering the fundamental empirical question: What is going on here? Brewer and Jones (2002).

McKenzie, Sallis and Nadar (1991) and Rowe, Schuldheisz, and van der Mars, (1997) explain that although research has been conducted on fitness levels and participation levels in youth sport, there has been very little, if any, research based around the coaching behaviours of youth football coaches and the content delivered to participants during a practice session. Therefore, within this study, by observing coaching behaviour and session content coupled together with analyzing these topics with existing skills and attributes which the coaches possess, a more accurate conclusion can be made to see if there are any relationships between these categories. Furthermore, because it is suggested that formal education and coach specific education are factors which can affect a coaches behaviour, and because this research study is specific to youth football coaches, an area which will be analysed in more depth will be if there is any relationship between the formal football qualifications gained from a football coach and how a coach behaves during delivery of a coaching session.

The purpose of this study was to determine if there are any relationships between coaches' behaviour, the experience, education, football qualifications gained and the content which is being delivered in training sessions. Therefore, the research objectives (RO) for this study are as follows:

- **RO 1** - Through the analysis of systematic observation of youth football coaches, the purpose of this study was to determine if there were any relationships between coaches behaviour, the experience, education, football qualifications gained and the content which is being delivered in training sessions.

2.0 Literature Review

This chapter critically analyses existing literature and research which is associated with coaching behaviours in sport. Gratton and Jones (2004) explain that the literature review provides an outline of the relevant theories and concepts important within a research project. Although this chapter aims to analyse other work, theories and concepts which have been written around this study's topic, it also aims to compare and contrast associations made between the studies. Gratton and Jones (2004) continue to state that a literature review will help create a hypothesis where a predicted outcome can be reached based around the research which has gone before it based upon logical reason or existing evidence. The primary research objective for this study is to determine if there are any relationships between the ways various coaches behave, the experience and education which the coaches have received and, the context in which the sessions are delivered therefore impacting on the content which the participants receive.

In order for the research objectives to be met, relevant past studies were reviewed and analysed. With the study being based around variable outcomes of systematic observations, the literature focuses on a number of areas. For example, the area of study is based around systematic observation therefore other studies which involved the kind of instruments used in this study (Arizona State University Observation Instrument and System for Observing Fitness Instruction Time) were reviewed. However, as the coaches were profiled using six different categories, literature surrounding coach education and development was also reviewed. Key authors for this study included Gallimore & Tharpe, and Potrac, Jones and Armour in regards to systematic observations and, Cushion with regards to coach education and development.

Tharp and Gallimore (1976) conducted the first descriptive study of systematic observation on a coach; they intended to provide information on the coaching behaviour of a successful collegiate basketball coach. Initial results revealed that the coach spent a high percentage of his practice time (over 50%) in some form of instructional behaviour. Miller (1992) explains that since the coach involved was a highly successful coach and his practice breakdown consisted of a high percentage of time devoted to instruction, a future line of research began that examined what type of coaching behaviours other successful coaches exhibited. Langsdorf (1979), Dodds and Rife (1981), and Lacy and Darst (1985) interestingly, all showed during their research that the greatest percentage of time spent among the coaches was some form of instruction. However, although instruction is the predominant behaviour, their study shows absolutely no correlations between behaviour and content delivered. However, as their study only focuses on coach behaviour and not content, their studies do not present any indication of the kind of education or indeed the experiences the coaches had received, thus influencing their behaviour. Therefore, within this study, session content was observed and analysed to help gain a better understanding of what is actually being delivered in youth football coaching sessions.

Abraham and Collins (1998) insist that coaches' knowledge and action can be viewed as both the product and manifestation of a personally experienced involvement with the coaching process, this being the purposeful improvement of competition sports performance, achieved through a planned programme of preparation and competition Cross and Lyle (2000). Cross and Lyle (2000) continue to state that this knowledge is linked to the coaches' own histories and, crucially, are attributable to how they were learned. Therefore, although the early studies illustrate what coaches behaviour was like, there is no background information of the coaches. Furthermore, because Langsdorf (1979), Dodds and Rife (1981), and Lacy and Darst (1985) studies have focused on three different coaches at three different levels of coaching, for example: high school, collegiate and elite, perhaps then that there is a correlation between the different levels of coaching. However, there is no evidence throughout these studies of the qualifications or educational background of these coaches. Abraham and Collins (1998) say that coaching awards or certification are a common and traditional feature of coach education and now contain more information than ever, dealing with a range of issues from technique and tactics to elements of sport science. Therefore, it can be argued that by having more or higher qualifications, this would ensure a better coach education. However, these early studies do not show this and therefore it is impossible to conclude from this evidence if education influenced the coach's behaviour. Therefore, by profiling the coaches during this study, a distinction can be made if education or indeed experiences are key factors in the way a coach behaves and the content which is being delivered.

Claxton (1988) examined behaviour of more or less successful high school tennis coaches and found that less successful tennis coaches actually instructed more, 12% of intervals recorded, than the more successful coaches, 8% of intervals recorded. The 3 categories of instruction were the highest percentage behaviour categories' other than silence and "other" of the total intervals. Thus, if earlier studies have shown that instruction is the most used behaviour with successful coaches, Claxton's study clearly evidences that this is not necessarily a valid argument. Therefore, it could be argued that instructional behaviour only works within the realms of certain sports.

Research over the last decade has demonstrated that it is experience and the observation of other coaches that remain the primary sources of knowledge for coaches, yet despite this, coach education and continuing professional development fail to draw effectively on this experience (Gould, Gianinni, Krane and Hodge 1990, Salmela 1996, Cushion 2001, Gilbert and Trudel 2001, and Cushion, Armour and Jones 2003). Furthermore, Gould *et al* (1990), Salmela *et al* (1994) and Cushion *et al* (2003) also explain that observation of other coaches; experience and qualifications play a role in coaching behaviour. However, referring back to future development by Abraham and Collins (1998) stating that coaching awards or certification are a common and traditional feature of coach education and now contain more information than ever, this indicates that certification is a vital tool in coach education but should be combined with observations of other coaches. However, Cushion *et al* (2003) argue that if educational programs are to develop imaginative, dynamic, and thoughtful coaches, they must widen the search beyond the usual suspects of content knowledge that has informed coach education programs. Furthermore, Jones, Armour and Potrac (1998) insist that if coach education programs continue to focus on content then they will run the risk of simply having a modernised version of the same. Therefore, by profiling the coaches using the various categories including certification gained, the study will be able to gauge if certification and/or experience has influenced the coach's behaviour. Jones (2000) argues that coach education courses, having been developed along rationalistic lines, currently do not develop intellectual, and practical competencies, namely, independent and creative thinking skills in relation to meaning making and problem solving. Macdonald and Tinning (1995) and Potrac, Jones, Brewer, Armour and Hoff (2000) agree and state that by separating theory from practice in educational courses, high level tasks have been presented as sequential routine, which has resulted in the deskilling of the practitioner in terms of cognitive and human interaction.

Gilbert, Cote and Mallet (2006) and Werthner and Trudel (2006) explain that although there are many different behaviours used during a coaching session, other factors outside of the coaching process and educational programs can influence these behaviours. Rodgers, Reade and Hall (2007) explain that age and sex of the coach, the coach's years of experience, their levels of formal education and coach specific education, as well as their competitive background, for example personal involvement as an athlete, could all be factors why the coach behaves in such a manner.

Other systematic observation studies on coaches were conducted by Smith, Smoll, and Hunt (1978), Lacy (1989) and, Rupert and Buschner (1989) which indicated a high amount of practice time devoted to instruction. Lacy (1989) study observed youth sport soccer coaches and found that the dominant coaching behaviour exhibited was again some form of instruction, 34% of the recorded intervals, with management second at 23% of the recorded intervals. The third most dominant behaviour category was the combination of the percent of intervals of praise and hustles. These categories contributed almost 10% to the total. It should be noted also that the praise to scold ratio during Lacy (1989) study was 6.7 to 1.5 denoting that youth sport soccer coaches spend a higher percent of intervals reinforcing correct behaviour than scolding inferior behaviour. Once again, during this study there is no indication on the success of the youth coaches, nor does it mention the content which was being delivered or the context in which it was delivered. Furthermore, there is no evidence to show what impact these behaviours had on the participants nor does it highlight the coach's experience or educational pathways. Therefore, during this study the coaches will be profiled to highlight what type of coach id doing what during the training sessions.

Schmidt (1988) and Lee, Keh and Magill (1993) state that effective coaching instruction is an essential component, however a proficient coach needs a variety of pedagogical skills. Although it is recognized that instruction is still an important component of coaching it could be argued that this instruction is inadequate without further skills.

Referring back to the studies conducted by Smith *et al* (1978), Lacy *et al* (1989) and, Rupert *et al* (1989), they concluded that the behaviour category of silence received the highest individual percentage of recorded intervals with 28.52%. Therefore, although instruction was the highest used behaviour in previous studies with successful coaches, it does appear that silence is also one of the most common behaviours in coaching. This is in agreement with previous studies from (Tharp and Gallimore, 1976; Langsdorf, 1979; Dodds and Rife, 1981; Lacy and Darst, 1985; Lacy, 1988; and Claxton, 1988) which shows there is no indication of how experienced the coaches were, what education they had received or indeed how effective the sessions were in regards to the content which the participants received. Therefore, it could be suggested that these earlier studies hold insufficient information to allow for an accurate understanding of coaching behaviour. For example, although these early studies illustrate how a coach behaves, they do not give a deeper concept of other factors which could have influenced their behaviour.

Despite evidence supporting the need for instruction, studies from Rupert *et al* (1989) in an observational study of nine teacher/coaches and Smith and Cushion (2006) in a study involving elite youth soccer coaches have also showed that silence was the highest category used. In fact one of the coaches from Smith *et al's* (2006)study, when interviewed, explains that silence was necessary by the coaches to observe and analyse, and was used as a method to encourage the players to learn for themselves, the coach involved explains, 'I want the players to learn themselves. I don't want prescribed motions of play. The kids have got to learn, finding out through their own learning experiences, success, OK and negatives or not successful'. Furthermore, in Smith *et al's* (2006) study a second coach talks about the impact instruction can have on children when delivering a training session, the coach explains, 'give instruction but not overwhelm the kids with instruction, you can't take everything in all at once. So I try and keep it simple, especially the younger ones and as clear as possible'. Once again, although instruction has been proven in past studies to be a useful behaviour for successful coaching, it would appear that in more current studies silence is shown to be more appropriate. However, although there appears to be a conflict in what behaviours are successful and beneficial to participants, there is still no evidence to show what has influenced these behaviours. Furthermore, if instruction has been such a dominant behaviour in past studies, there is absolutely no evidence to illustrate within these studies what verbal instruction was given.

Cushion, Armour and Jones (2006) explain that although there has been much research recorded quantitatively using observational instruments, these studies would have benefitted from additional qualitative research to gain an understanding of why the coaches behaved the way they did during these sessions. Furthermore, although systematic observations have been carried out on coaching behaviour, very little study has been conducted on the participant's involvement during youth soccer practices.

Clear evidence has been presented through past studies Smith, Smoll, and Hunt (1978), Langsdorf (1979), Dodds and Rife (1981), Lacy and Darst (1985), Claxton (1988), Lacy (1989) and, Rupert and Buschner (1989) that coaching behaviours can differ from sport to sport and indeed affect the success the coaches achieve.

McKenzie, Sallis and Nadar (1991) and Rowe, Schuldheisz, and van der Mars, (1997) explain that although research has been conducted on fitness levels and participation levels in youth sport, there has been very little, if any, research based around the coaching behaviours of youth football coaches and the content delivered to participants during a practice session. Interestingly, coaching practice, and in particularly coach behaviour, and player learning has been the centre of The English FA in recent times, Brooking (2006 p. 2) explains:

> "We know that a lot of youngsters still experience very old fashioned training sessions, with very little emphasis on ball skills. These courses will hopefully supplement some of the practical knowledge coaches learn on a Level 1 or Level 2 coaching course, but also ensure that the coaches make sessions fun and enjoyable. We have to change the coaching philosophy in this country, particularly with the 5-11 age group, and focus on getting children to feel comfortable on the ball, and stop coaches shouting instructions and interrupting sessions; it's about making learning fun."

Brooking makes it perfectly clear that shouting instructions should be kicked out of youth football coaching sessions; therefore it would appear that indeed the coaching behaviour of youth football coaches should be changed. However, it must be noted that this is only one man's opinion and therefore cannot be judged as a profound or indeed accurate statement.

Within the parameters of sport and physical education some studies have been carried out on what coaches and players do, however, this facet of research remains largely unexplored, (Lacy and Martin 1994). Potrac, Jones and Armour (2002) also agree and state that despite the increasing recognition that coaching is vulnerable to differing contextual pressures and constraints, it is considered that the sociological analysis of coaching practice to be largely underdeveloped and an under-researched area. Potrac *et al* (2002) continue to say that the constant production of articles since 1975 focusing on different aspects of coach behaviour in varying sports, would appear to indicate that direct observation of coaches is an appropriate method for describing coaches' behaviour in training and competition. Moreover, the studies conducted to date, using various observation instruments, have given insights that have contributed greatly to the body of knowledge in sport pedagogy DeMarco, Mancini, Wuest and Schempp (1996). Although research into coaching has increased incredibly over the past 20 years, an area of neglect has been that of the youth football coach, Smith *et al* (2006).

3.0 Methodology

3.1 Introduction

This chapter evaluates and justifies the rationale behind the methods used to achieve the study's objectives. The main research aim is to identify any relationships between coaching behaviours and the content which is being delivered and whether key educational or experiential factors affect these outcomes. Youth football coaches are observed for the purpose of this study and the data recorded will be used to analytically measure any correlations between the variable factors ensuring that the following research objectives (RO) are closely examined:

- **RO 1** - Through the analysis of systematic observation of youth football coaches, the purpose of this study was to determine if there were any relationships between coaches behaviour, the experience, education, football qualifications gained and the content which is being delivered in training sessions.

3.2 Philosophical Paradigm

This study observes human behaviour and, more specifically, football coaches and participants behaviour. Gratton and Jones (2004) explain that when researching human behaviour a positivist approach is necessary where the principles and methods are objective and tangible in nature, such as statistics, as opposed to an interpretive approach where words, statements and other non-numerical measures are interpreted by the researcher. Gratton and Jones (2004) continue by insisting that this kind of research allows for results which can be used to predict future behaviour and/or to rectify particular problems within the area of study. Thomas, Nelson and Silverman (2005) state that statistics is simply an objective means of interpreting a collection of observations. Therefore, the results collected from the observations of this particular study, not only illustrate the behaviours of football coaches and what is happening during these sessions but the data can be used as a foundation for further and more detailed research. Furthermore, as the research being undertaken for this study is looking at what factors can affect a football coaching session, precise control and measurement was needed. Gratton and Jones

(2004) explain that using a positivist approach has its undoubted strengths because of its precision, control and objectivity. Because of the numerical data collection which is involved during this research, a quantitative approach will be used. This will allow measurable quantities to be analysed, for example the number of times the coach praises a player or the number of minutes the participants have engaged in game play, presented and discussed with a view to be used in further research. Furthermore, quantitative research allowed the categories to be directly measured Gratton and Jones (2004). For example, with the coaches being profiled using five different categories and with thirteen different behaviour categories, the quantitative research allowed for these categories to be measured and converted into numerical form, thus statistical analysis could be performed.

3.3 Sample

The samples selected were separated into two categories; coaches and participants. Firstly, for logistical purposes and time constraints, the coaches selected consisted of volunteer youth football coaches from the South Liverpool Football League. A presentation to all prospective coaches was delivered during a committee meeting of a South Liverpool Football League Football Club; this enabled the research to recruit the appropriate coaches.

Coaches

The sample group was of mixed gender and their coach education and experience varied. Previous research on coaching expertise has used a combination of several criteria to determine the appropriate coaches for study Cote, Salmela and Russell (1995); these criteria included the number of years of coaching experience and officially recognized qualifications and skills, Cote *et al* (1995). Following on from cote *et al* research criterion, the coaches' were profiled by using the following categories: coaching experience, playing experience, English FA coaching qualifications, further education and age group which they coached., table 1.0 shows the quantities for each category, this information was compiled through questionnaires, see appendix 1.0.

Participants

Secondly, the participants of the coaching sessions were children aged between five – 14 years old and were categorized and divided into the following age groups, table 1.2 illustrates this. The participants were part of a team, playing and training regularly together, and were coached by the same coach each week giving them familiarity both with their coach and their coach's style. Gratton and Jones (2004) insist that when sampling, the population must be representative of the particular study. A number of sampling strategies are available and for the purpose of this study systematic sampling is used. Gratton and Jones continue to explain systematic sampling as using the *n*th case. Thomas, Nelson and Silverman (2005) and Tenenbaum and Driscoll (2005) insist that systematic sampling occurs when there are too many people or items to observe and therefore system is put into place to help choose the samples which represent the population. For the purpose of consistency throughout the study, three players from each training session at different intervals will be systematically chosen for observation. The criteria for this was the coaches register list for the participants, for example; Player one to be observed will be the player who is at the top of the register, player two will be the player whose name is fourth on the register and player three will be the player who is seventh on the register, and for easy identification for the observers, different coloured vests were worn by the chosen participants. Table 1.2 illustrates the number of observations which took place for each age group category. Furthermore, a diary and timetable of observations were kept and regularly updated to allow the researcher to plan accordingly. Furthermore, the diary will allow the research to be identically replicated, see appendix 1.1.

Table 1.1 Coach Profile.

GENDER		AGE GROUP COACHED		COACHING QUALIFICATIONS		PLAYING EXPERIENCE		COACHING EXPERIENCE		FURTHER EDUCATION	
		AGE	NO. OF COACHES	LEVEL	NO. OF COACHES	NO. OF YEARS	NO. OF COACHES	NO. OF YEARS	NO. OF COACHES	OTHER QUALS.	NO. OF COACHES
M	14	U7	4	1	10	0-5	0	0-2	0	GCSE'S	4
F	0	U8	0	2	4	5-10	0	2-5	6	A LEVEL	6
		U9	5	3	0	10-15	4	5-7	2	DEGREE	4
		U10	2			+15	10	+7	6	MASTERS	0
		U11	0							PHD	0
		U12	1								
		U13	2								
		U14	0								

Table 1.2 Participant Samples.

AGE GROUP	NUMBER OF TEAMS AT THIS AGE GROUP	NUMBER OF OBSERVATIONS TAKEN WITH THIS AGE GROUP
U7	2	4
U8	0	0
U9	2	5
U10	1	2
U11	0	0
U12	1	1
U13	1	2
U14	0	0

Dave Earnden

3.4 Instruments

The instruments used for this investigation were the Arizona State University Observation Instrument (ASUOI), see appendix 1.1 and an adapted version of System for Observing Fitness Instruction Time (SOFIT), see appendix 1.2 (for the purpose of this study and to allow for easy interpretation, the adapted version will be referred to as SOCAB System for Observing practice Content And coach Behaviour), see appendix 1.3. Potrac, Jones and Cushion (2007) explain that the ASUOI instrument was designed to collect information on the behaviours of coaches in the practice environment using a ten category system originally developed and designed by Tharp and Gallimore (1976) for systematically observing coach behaviour within a coaching setting. McKenzie, Sallis and Nadar (1991) describe SOFIT as a direct observation instrument designed to assess variables associated with students' activity levels. McKenzie *et al* (1991) continue to explain that SOFIT involves the systematic observation of physical education classes while simultaneously recording student physical activity levels, curriculum context variables, and teacher behaviour. However, because of the purpose of this study where physical activity levels are not being observed and analysed, the SOFIT instrument had to be adapted.

Dave Earnden

Table 1.3 Definitions of categories for SOCAB

Session Context	Definition
General Training (**G**)	Includes warm up and introduction to topic where no formal, technical coaching is involved.
Technical Play (**T**)	Involves individual technique where no direct or passive pressure is added to player, allows player to be comfortable learning a new technique with no pressure, includes individual ball manipulation and will include formal coaching.
Skill Play (**S**)	Progresses from individual technique to allowing passive pressure and some direct pressure from other player/s, includes decision making (when and where to use technique), formal coaching should be used.
Modified/Topic Related Game Play (**P**)	Develops technical aspect and the decision making aspect into a purposeful, goal oriented, modified game. Direct pressure only should be evident throughout; coaching should be used during this category.
Conditioned Small Sided Game	Should be structured by the coach and conditions introduced

(V)	which relate to session topic. Typical numbers used during this aspect will be 3v3, 4v4, 5v5, 6v6 or above. Coaching should be evident throughout this element.
Free Play **(F)**	Participants play small sided game with no conditions attached nor will there be any coaching elements involved.
Other **(O)**	If none of the above can be recognised during the sessions then this category should be used.

The SOCAB instrument had been specifically adapted to assist in systematically observing lesson content. The new categories introduced to observe the content of the session were the following: general training, technical play, skill play, modified/topic related game play, conditioned small sided game and free play, definitions for each category have been described, see table 1.3). The categories were carefully chosen so that it could accurately illustrate the content and structure of the session. It can be argued that structured sessions in football are the best way to learn. Ex-professional footballer and coach Upson cited in The FA (2006 p. 1) explains “As a player you benefit most from sessions which are structured and help you to gain experience, whatever position you play”.

3.5 Procedure

To help establish if SOCAB was a viable instrument for this study, three pilot observations were held prior to the research. Six football practice sessions which lasted for approximately one hour were observed. The location of these pilots was at a local playing field in the South Liverpool area. The first five minutes and last five minutes were not logged as this time allowed for a general warm up and cool down, only the statistics gained from the 50 minutes in between were logged. The sessions were observed by two independent people who had been trained how to use the instrument. After each session the data were compared and analysed to ensure that each observer's data were accurate with each other. Once the pilot study had been authenticated, 20 practice sessions were observed with each coach and their respective team being observed twice. The times of the coaching session varied quite substantially as were the locations of the practices. However, for the purpose of this study the variables which were encountered during these sessions perhaps provided a more realistic generalization of how football practices are delivered within the South Liverpool area. The observations for each coach had a four week gap between each session to allow for discrepancies with improvement in both coach and participant, thus providing more accurate and reliable data. Each coach delivered an hour long session and will be observed twice with a four week interval in between each observation. The first five minutes and last five minutes will not be logged as this time will allow for a general warm up and cool down, only the statistics gained from the 50 minutes in between will be logged. These data was taken during a live session with no video tape being used to clarify these findings. However, the coaches and participants were observed by two different, independent parties who were trained how to use each observational instrument; one who will use the ASUOI and the other using SOCAB.

3.6 Data Analysis & Further Research

- **Quantitative Data Analysis**

The analysis techniques used for data collected were dependent upon a number of different factors including the type of research question, the number of dependent and independent variables and also the existence of covariates. The analysis relied predominantly on descriptive statistics in order to satisfy the purpose of the research and also to maximise the value of the information gained.

The first stage of the data analysis was to explore whether the data was normally distributed in order to be able to use a mean score or whether a median value was the accurate statistic to use, Pallant (2004). This was done through histograms to check if the distribution lacked symmetry or pointyness, Field (2005). Although the statistics used were descriptive, it was still important to consider thoroughly checking normality were necessary which involved following up histograms with Kolmogorov-Smirnov tests, Field (2005). This then was used to determine whether a parametric or non-parametric test was carried out. In testing the data, it is assumed that the populations of the samples have equal variances Pallant (2004).

The study used mainly non parametric tests, mainly due to parametric assumptions being violated. These included Friedman's ANOVA to explore differences between several related groups, Field (2005); Independent Samples T-test and Mann Whitney U tests (comparison of two independent conditions, Field (2005). As aforementioned, descriptive statistics were heavily relied on because of the nature and approach of the study. This was mainly achieved through frequency and percentage counts displayed in graphical form which was followed up with the relevant non parametric tests were deemed relevant.

3.7 Ethical Consideration

Essentially the research method was systematic observation where children were involved and therefore appropriate duty of care of the children was necessary. However, because the youth teams were part of a football club, ethical clearance was achieved through the football club itself, see appendix 1.4 for a copy of this agreement. Furthermore, complete confidentiality and anonymity was adhered to when observing, analysing and commenting on the coaches who were involved. Gratton and Jones (2004) and Thomas, Nelson and Silverman (2005) insist that good ethical practice should consist of all participants involved being informed as to who will have access to the research data. Thus, each coach was advised of this information and numbers of people who had access to the data were restricted to the researcher and professional advocates and advisers of the researcher.

3.8 Validity and Reliability

The research carried out for this study details the validity of different observational instruments, System for Observing Fitness Instruction Time (SOFIT) and the adapted version SOCAB and, Arizona State University Observation Instrument (ASUOI) as well as looking at coaching behaviour and player participation.

Furthermore, it looked at whether coach's behaviour can affect the engagement levels of player participation and the content of a coaching session. McKenzie, Sallis and Nadar (1991) claim that because of the ease of using the instrument, the short time required to train observers and the evidence of construct validity in their sample suggest that SOFIT is suitable for investigating physical activity and fitness development opportunities for students. Therefore, because of the ease of use, the SOFIT instrument was chosen to be adapted to observe and analyse the coaching content and participation levels. However, to ensure that the adapted version was suitable a pilot study had to be conducted which is described within the procedure. The pilot study proved to be reliable for this research, however, it is not subject to being a valid instrument, further in-depth research studies would be needed to validate the instrument. Rowe, Schuldheisz, and van der Mars (1997) validate the SOFIT instrument insisting that the activity categories indicate different levels of energy expenditure, whereas the sitting and lying categories refer to the same energy level expenditure.

To help with validation of SOFIT, McKenzie, Stone, Feldman, Epping, Yang, Strikmiller, Lytle and Parcel (2001) had trained their observers classroom trained, used videotape analysis, field practice and certification assessments. Their accuracy was measured periodically through the coding of pre-coded videotapes. Potrac, Jones and Cushion (2007) explain that before their final research and observations took place, they ran a pilot study before their main research commenced and found that ASUOI and its behavioural categories were adequately comprehensive and reflective of coaching behaviours. However, Potrac *et al* (2007) do conclude within their study that systematic observation has been the subject of some criticism as many have highlighted its weakness in favouring more qualitative approaches. However, Potrac *et al* believe that this type of research can work in conjunction and perhaps compliment the already established qualitative research methods. Therefore, although this study successfully observed and analysed coaching behaviour, perhaps further qualitative research would compliment this particular study.

3.9 Limitations

Although relationships were found between the varying profiles of the coaches, coaching behaviour and session content, it could be argued that more instruments or indeed a mix of research methods would be needed to make this study more specific. For example, by including a qualitative approach to the study, it would allow for an understanding of why the coaches behaved the way that they did. Holborn and Langley (2004) explain that a qualitative approach tends to be richer and has more depth. Furthermore, Holborn and Langley (2004) assert that qualitative data is used to interpret social action with an emphasis on the meanings and motives. Therefore, by using this method in conjunction with this study a bigger and better understanding can be reached. Further limitations regarding the instruments used also occurred during this study. For example, due to time restrictions and logistical implications only two instruments were used. Although these instruments provided quality and accurate data, it could be argued that the data limited the study. For example, the ASUOI instrument only monitored the coach's type of behaviour; it did not record exactly what was being said during the sessions. Although the coach may have appeared to be giving instruction to the participants ASUOI does not state exactly what was said during that instruction. More, McGarry, Partridge and Franks (1996) used the Coach Analysis Instrument which is an instrument used to systematically examine the effectiveness of verbal coaching behaviour and to record verbal content from a coach. Therefore, had more time been allocated and extra observers been assigned to the project, this instrument could certainly have enhanced the research and would have helped in giving a broader insight to coaching behaviour. However, although there were limitations to this particular study, the information and data recorded was certainly sufficient enough to achieve the research objectives of finding relationships between the ways various coaches behave and the context in which the sessions are delivered therefore impacting on the content which the participants receive.

Dave Earnden

4.0 Results

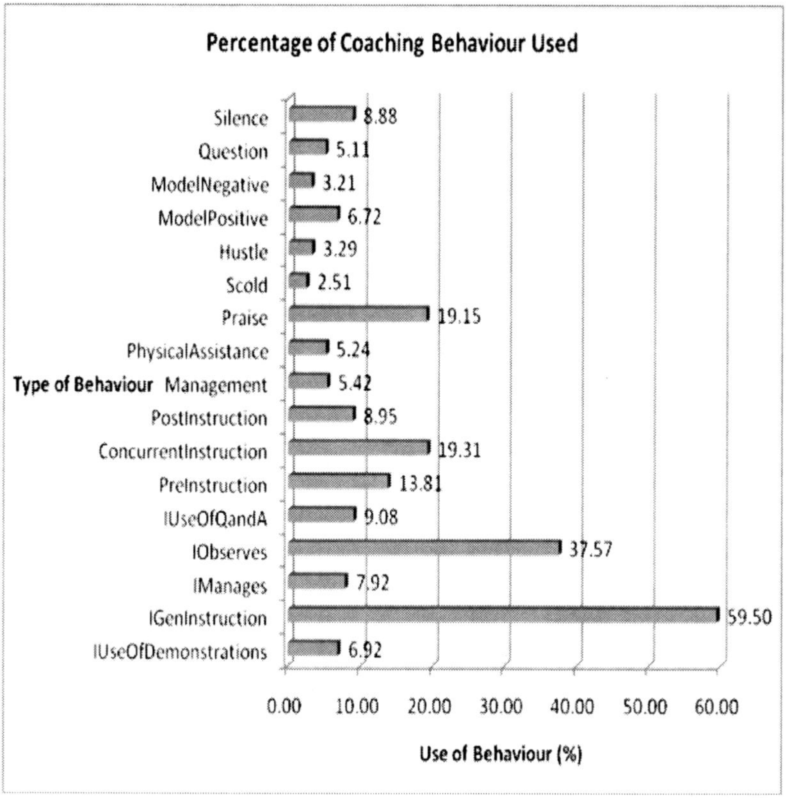

Figure 1.1 Percentage of coaching behaviour used

General instruction (m = 59.50%) was found to be the most commonly used behaviour with scold (m = 2.51%) scoring the least. Out of the three types of instruction, concurrent instruction (m = 19.31%) scored highest with post instruction (m = 8.95%) scoring the least. When not including instruction, observation (m = 37.75%) and praise (m = 19.15%) scored the highest.

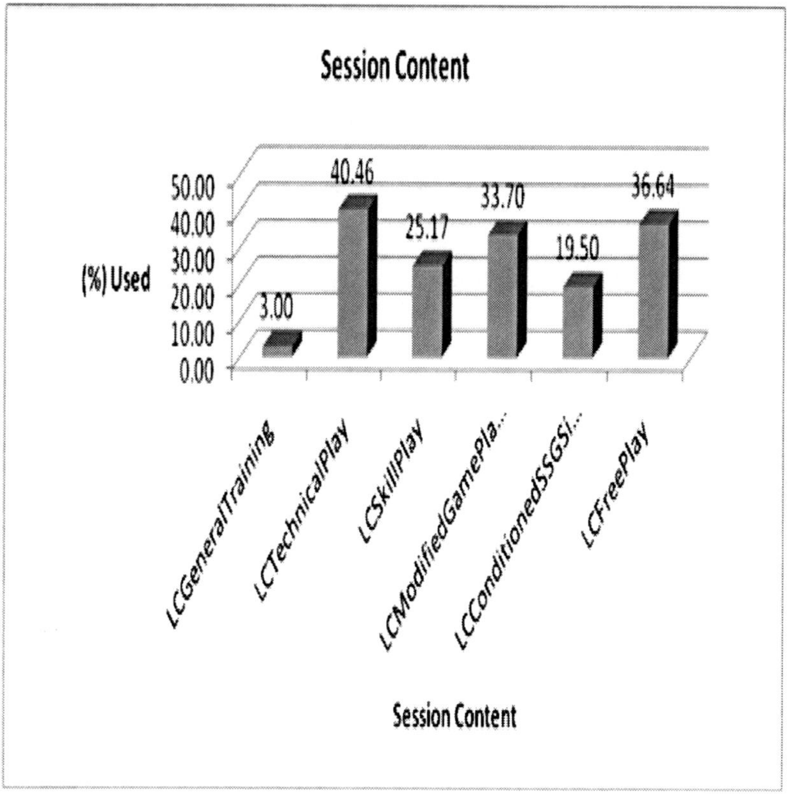

Figure 1.2 Session content delivered

Technical play (m = 40.46%) and free play (m = 36.64%) scored highest in types of content used during a session with general training (m = 3%) and other (m = 7.05%) scoring the lowest. Conditioned small sided game scored lowest with (m = 19.50%) if the categories other and general training were not counted.

Table 1.4 Percentage of time spent in use of behaviour by level of coaching certificate

Behaviour Type	FA Level 1(%)	FA Level 2 (%)	Total (%)
Silence	6.26	15.43	8.88
Question	4.14	7.53	5.11
Model Negative	2.61	3.96	3.21
Model Positive	4.96	11.11	6.72
Hustle	3.53	2.68	3.29
Scold	2.73	1.41	2.51
Praise	19.86	17.38	19.15
Physical Assistance	4.65	7.00	5.24
Management	6.74	2.13	5.42
Post Instruction	9.67	7.13	8.95
Concurrent Instruction	20.85	15.44	19.31
Pre-Instruction	14.90	11.09	13.81
Use of Q&A	6.56	14.75	9.08
Observes	34.60	45.00	37.57
Manages	9.50	4.75	7.92
General Instruction	64.80	46.25	59.50
Use of Demonstrations	6.67	7.50	6.92

General instruction scored highest for both FA Level 1 coaches (m = 64.80%) and FA Level 2 coaches (m = 46.25%). Concurrent instruction (m = 19.31%) scored highest out of all instruction types with FA Level 1 coaches (m = 20.85%) scoring higher than FA Level 2 coaches (m = 15.44%). Use of silence by FA Level 2 coaches (m = 15.43%) scored more than double the use of FA Level 1 coaches (m = 6.26%). The use of praise was scored highest by FA Level 1 coaches (m = 19.86%) than that of FA Level 2 coaches (m = 17.38%). Use of Q&A by FA Level 2 coaches (m = 14.75%) scored more than double the use of FA Level 1 coaches (m = 6.56%).

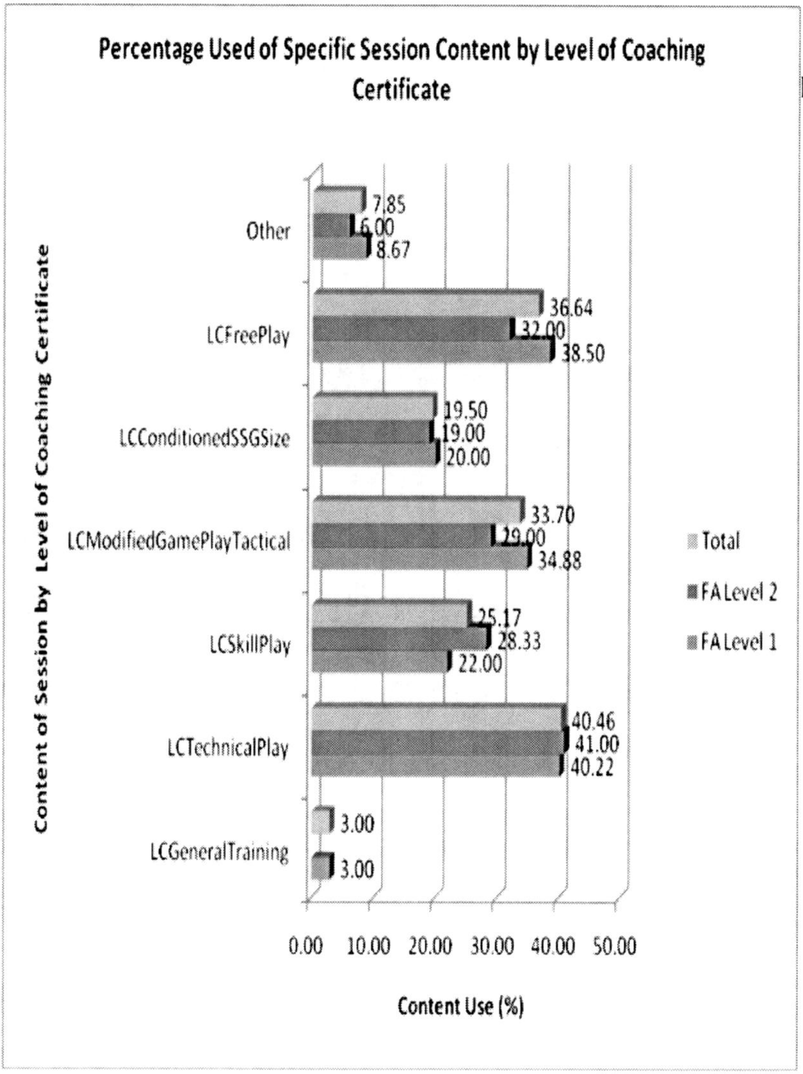
Percentage Used of Specific Session Content by Level of Coaching Certificate
Other
7.85
6.00
8.67
LCFreePlay
36.64
32.00
38.50
LCConditionedSSGSize
19.50
19.00
20.00
LCModifiedGamePlayTactical
33.70
29.00
34.88
LCSkillPlay
25.17
28.33
22.00
LCTechnicalPlay
40.46
41.00
40.22
LCGeneralTraining
3.00
3.00
Content of Session by Level of Coaching Certificate
0.00 10.00 20.00 30.00 40.00 50.00
Content Use (%)
Total
FA Level 2
FA Level 1

Figure 1.3 Percentage used of specific session content by level of coaching certificate

Technical play was scored highest by both FA Level 1 coaches (m = 40.22%) and FA Level 2 coaches (m = 41.00%). General training scored the lowest with only FA Level 1 coaches scoring (m = 3.00%). When other and general categories are not included conditioned SSG scored the lowest from both FA Level 1 coaches (m = 20.00%) and FA Level 2 coaches (m = 19.00%). Free play scored second highest with both FA Level 1 coaches (m = 38.50%) and FA Level 2 coaches (m = 32.00%). However, FA Level 2 coaches used modified game play tactical (m = 34.88%) more than what FA Level 1 coaches used free play (m = 32.00%).

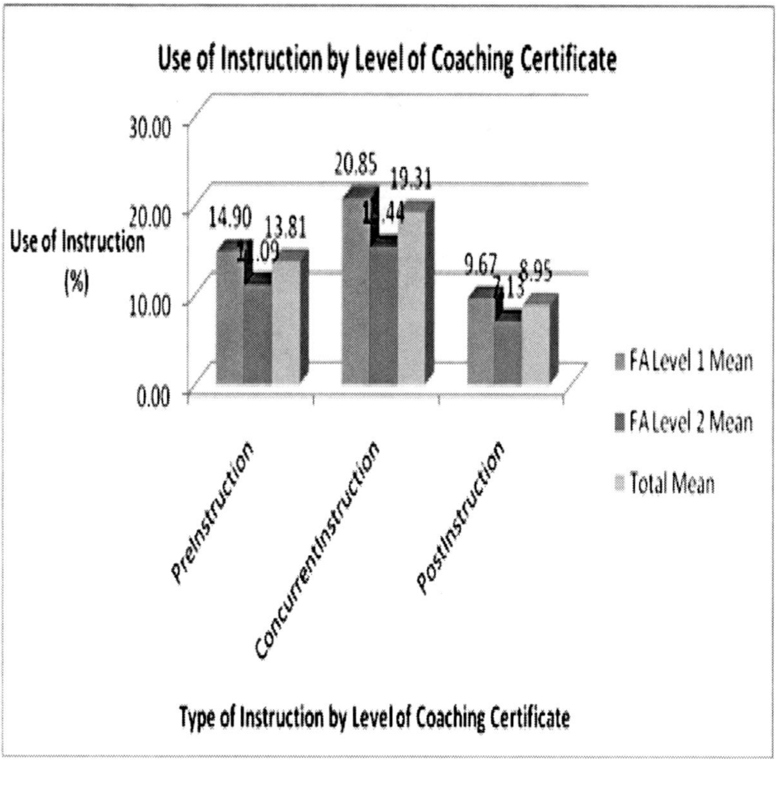

Figure 1.4 Use of instruction by level of coaching certificate

Concurrent instruction was the highest use of instruction by FA Level 1(m = 20.85%) and FA Level 2 (m = 15.44%) coaches with post instruction being used the least, FA Level 1(m = 9.67%) and FA Level 2 (m = 7.14%). The combined total for use of instruction for all coaches was (m = 14.02%).

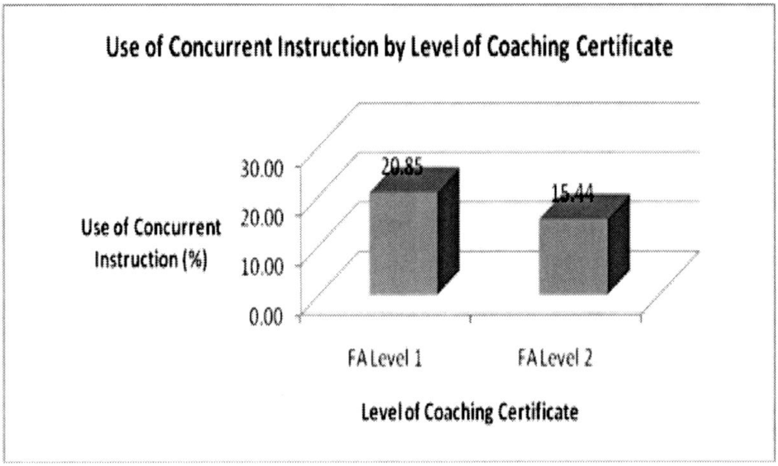

Figure 1.5 Use of concurrent instruction by level of coaching certificate

The data set violated parametric assumptions Level of Coaching Certification; (*D* (10) = 0.200, p>0.05). Therefore in order to explore relationships amongst the variables between FA level one coaches and FA level two coaches from use of concurrent instruction. Although an Independent Samples T-test showed that FA Level 1 Certificated Coaches (mean = 20.85 ± 6.33) scored higher than FA Level 2 Certificated Coaches (15.44 ± 4.31) in demonstrating use of concurrent instruction, this difference was not significant (t = 1.84, p = 0.101).

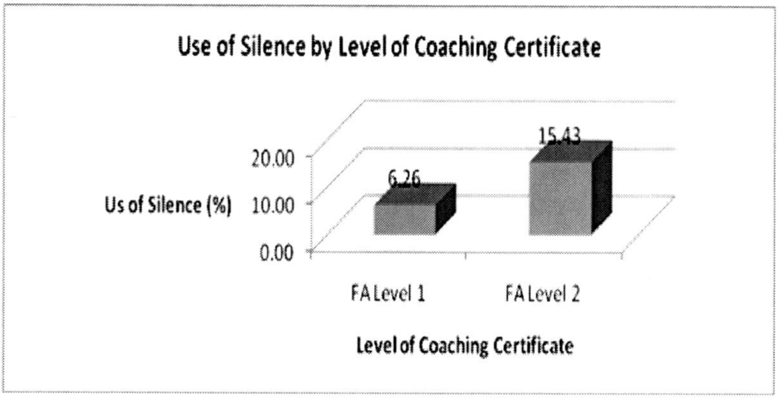

Figure 1.6 Use of silence by level of coaching certificate

The data set violated parametric assumptions Level of Coaching Certification; (*D* (10) = 0.116, p>0.05). Therefore in order to explore relationships amongst the variables between FA level one coaches and FA level two coaches from use of silence. An Independent Samples T-test showed that FA Level 2 Certificated Coaches (mean = 15.43 ± 4.91) scored higher than FA Level 1 Certificated Coaches (6.26 ± 3.84) in demonstrating use of silence, this difference was significant (t = -3.745, p = 0.024).

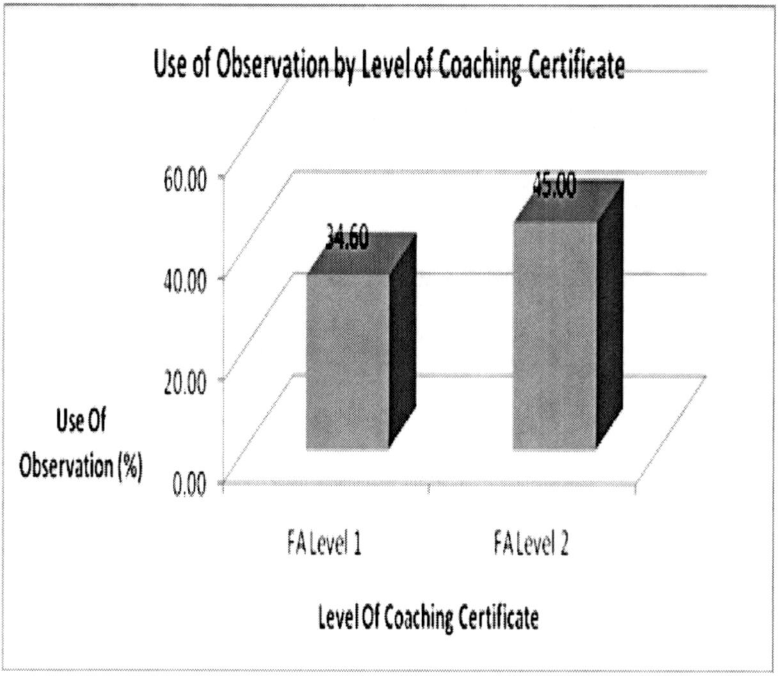

Figure 1.7 Use of observation by level of coaching certificate

The data set violated parametric assumptions Level of Coaching Certification; (*D* (10) = 0.200, $p>0.05$). Therefore in order to explore relationships amongst the variables between FA level one coaches and FA level two coaches from use of observation. Although an Independent Samples T-test showed that FA Level 2 Certificated Coaches (mean = 45.00 ± 7.75) scored higher than FA Level 1 Certificated Coaches (34.60 ± 11.36) in demonstrating use of observing, this difference was not significant ($t = -1.969$, $p = 0.083$).

Table 1.4 Correlation between silence and observe

		Silence	**IObserves**
Silence	Pearson Correlation	1	.632(*)
	Sig. (2-tailed)		.015
	N	14	14
IObserves	Pearson Correlation	.632(*)	1
	Sig. (2-tailed)	.015	

	N	14	14

*Correlation is significant at the 0.05 level (2-tailed).

The relationship between silence (deemed as coach not offering any oral input to participants as well as being off task) and observes (deemed as the coach observing the session making use to analyse the session) was investigated using Pearson product-moment correlation coefficient. Preliminary analyses were performed to ensure no violation of the assumptions of normality, linearity and homoscedasticity. There was a strong, negative correlation between the two variables ($r = 39.94$, $n = 14$, $p < .0005$).

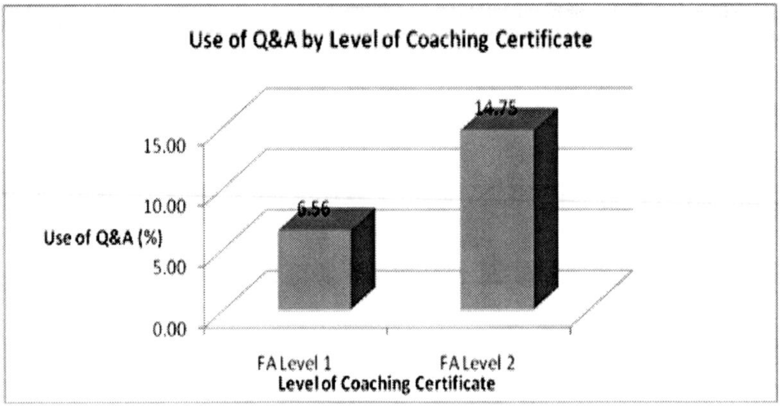

Figure 1.8 Use of Q&A by level of coaching certificate

The data set violated parametric assumptions Level of Coaching Certification; (*D* (9) = 0.200, p>0.05). Therefore in order to explore relationships amongst the variables between FA level one coaches and FA level two coaches from use of Q&A. An Independent Samples T-test showed that FA Level 2 Certificated Coaches (mean = 14.75

± 2.97) scored higher than FA Level 1 Certificated Coaches (6.56 ± 1.67) in demonstrating use of Q&A, this difference was significant ($t = -6.463$, $p = 0.007$).

Table 1.5 Percentage of time spent in coaching behaviour by Coaching Experience

Behaviour Type	2-5 Years (%)	5-7 Years (%)	7 Years Above (%)	Total (%)
Silence	7.79	18.88	6.63	8.88
Question	4.84	8.20	4.35	5.11
Model Negative	3.56	3.21	1.15	3.21
Model Positive	6.82	13.17	4.47	6.72
Hustle	2.67	3.56	3.81	3.29
Scold	2.07	2.10	2.94	2.51
Praise	19.89	13.17	20.41	19.15
Physical Assistance	6.81	3.62	3.68	5.24
Management	5.38	3.62	6.34	5.42
Post Instruction	5.86	8.52	12.18	8.95
Concurrent Instruction	20.77	13.59	19.75	19.31
Pre-Instruction	13.24	13.59	14.98	13.81
Use of Q&A	9.60	12.04	6.00	9.08
Observes	33.17	49.00	38.17	37.57
Manages	4.80	6.00	11.80	7.92
General Instruction	65.50	39.50	60.17	59.50
Use of Demonstrations	7.67	8.50	5.40	6.92

General instruction (m = 59.50%) scored highest with coaches with two – five years coaching experience scoring highest (m = 65.50%) and coaches with five – seven years experience scoring lowest (m = 39.50%), the second highest used behaviour was observes scoring (m = 37.57%). Coaches with two – five years experience (m = 20.77%) and coaches with seven years or above coaching experience (m = 19.75%) scored more than double of those coaches with five – seven years coaching experience using concurrent instruction. Coaches with two – five years coaching experience (m = 18.88%) scored almost three times as much as those with two – five years experience (m = 7.79%) and seven years or above coaching experience (m = 6.63%) in use of silence. Coaches with five – seven years coaching experience (m = 12.04%) scored double of those coaches with seven years or above coaching experience (m = 6.00%) in use of Q&A.

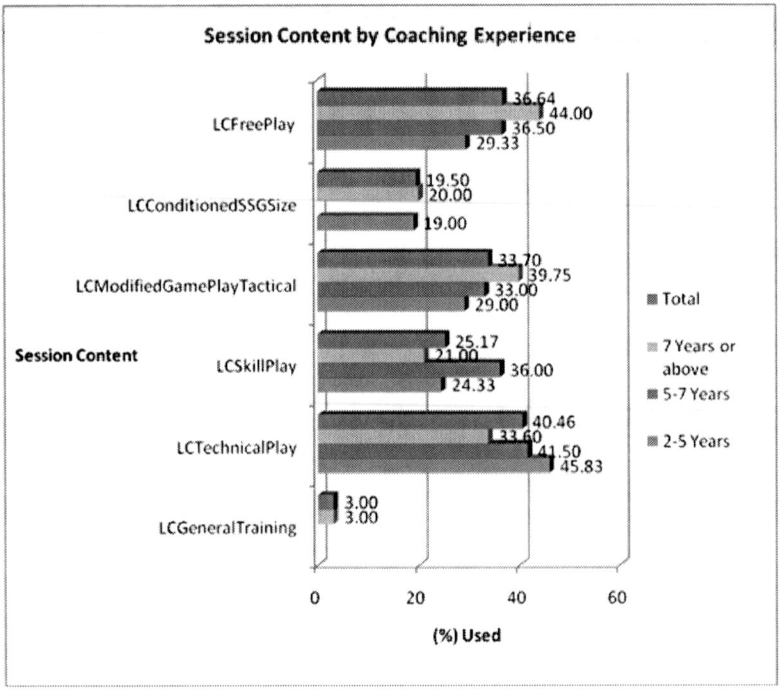

Figure 1.9 Session content by coaching experience

Technical play scored highest (m = 40.46%) with conditioned SSG scoring lowest (m = 19.50%).

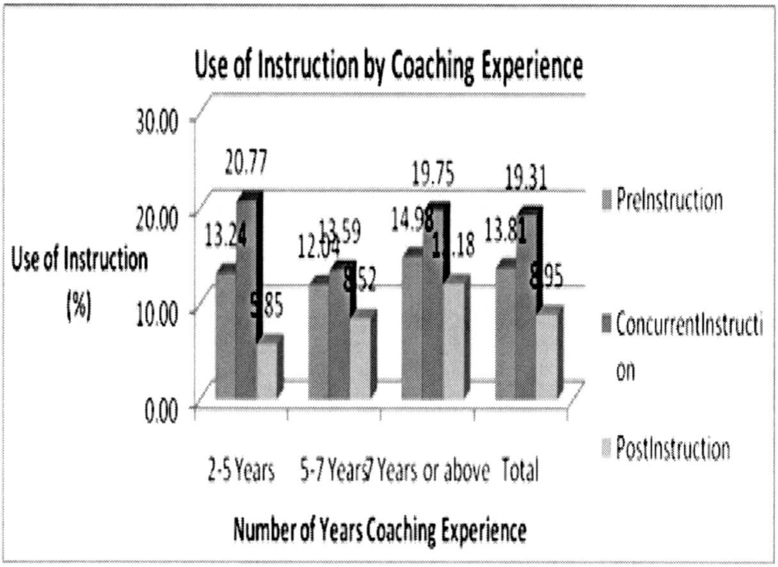

Figure 2.0 Use of instruction by coaching experience

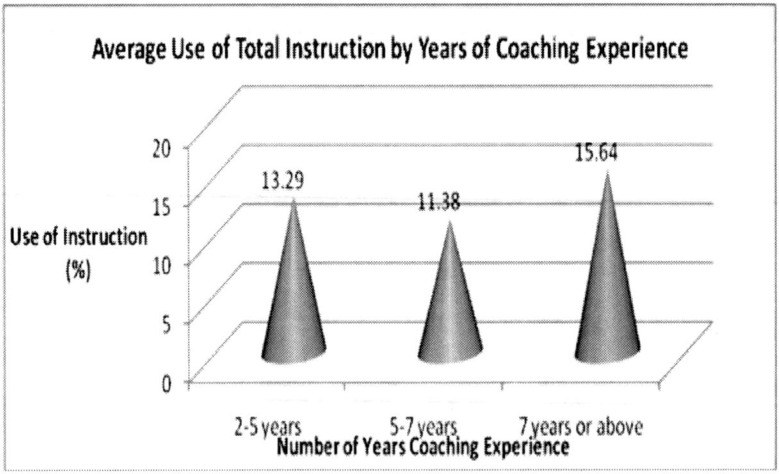

Figure 2.1 Average use of total instruction by years of coaching experience

Concurrent instruction was the highest use of instruction by all coaches from all categories of coaching experience with an average of (m = 19.31%). Post instruction was the least with an average of (m = 8.95%). Coaches that have seven years of experience or more showed a higher amount of instruction time (m = 15.64%) than those with two-five years experience (m = 13.29%) and those with five-seven years experience (m = 11.38%).

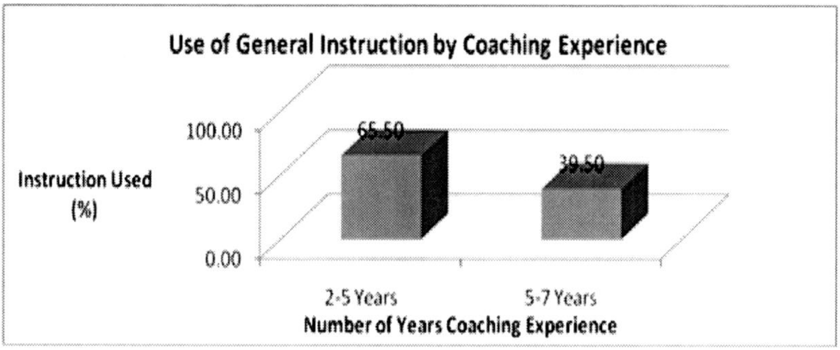

Figure 2.2 Use of general instruction by coaching experience

The data set violated parametric assumptions of Coaching Experience; (*D* (6) = 0.094, p>0.05). Therefore in order to explore relationships amongst the variables between coaches with two – five years coaching experience and coaches with five – seven years coaching experience from use of general instruction. An Independent Samples T-test showed that coaches with two – five years coaching experience (mean = 65.50 ± 10.15) scored higher than coaches with five – seven years experience (mean = 39.50 ± 2.12) in demonstrating use of general instruction, this difference was significant (t = 5.90, p = 0.14).

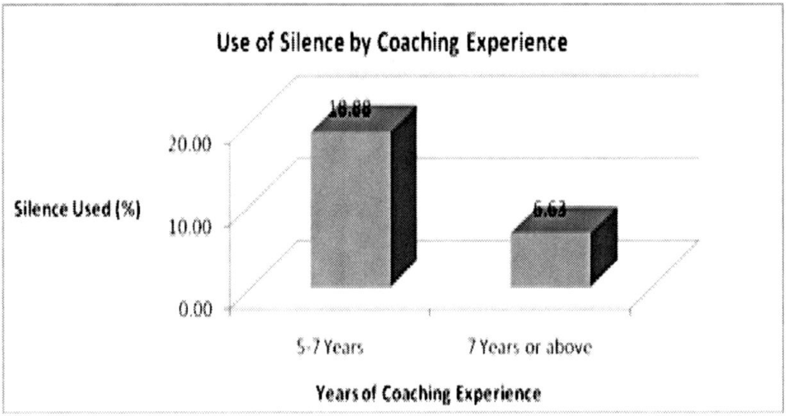

Figure 2.3 Use of silence by coaching experience

The data set violated parametric assumptions of Coaching Experience; (*D* (6) = 0.029, $p>0.05$). Therefore in order to explore relationships amongst the variables between coaches with five - seven years coaching experience and coaches with seven years or above coaching experience from use of silence. An Independent Samples T-test showed that Coaches with five – seven years coaching experience (mean = 18.88 ± 0.98) scored higher than Coaches with seven years or above experience (mean = 6.63 ± 4.36) in demonstrating use of silence, this difference was significant ($t = 6.41$, $p = 0.001$).

Table 1.6 Correlation between concurrent instruction and praise

		Concurrent Instruction	Praise
Concurrent Instruction	Pearson Correlation	1	.278
	Sig. (2-tailed)		.336
	N	14	14
Praise	Pearson Correlation	.278	1
	Sig. (2-tailed)	.336	
	N	14	14

The relationship between concurrent instruction and praise was investigated using Pearson product-moment correlation coefficient. Preliminary analyses were performed to ensure no violation of the assumptions of normality, linearity and homoscedasticity. There was a strong, negative correlation between the two variables ($r = 7.73$, $n = 14$, $p > .0005$).

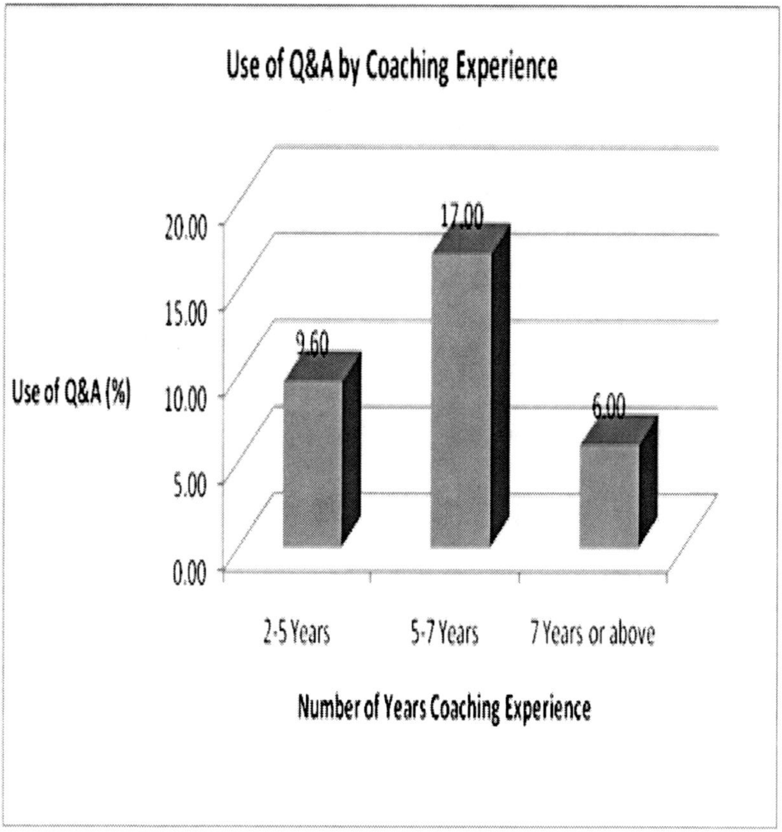

Figure 2.4 Use of Q&A by coaching experience

An Independent Samples T-test showed that coaches with 5-7 years of experience (mean = 17.00 ± 1.41) scored higher than coaches with 2-5 years of coaching experience (9.60 ± 2.88) in demonstrating use of Q&A,, this difference was significant ($t = -4.537$, $p = 0.009$) and was also higher than coaches with 7 years or above coaching experience (6.00 ± 1.79), this difference was also significant (8.88, $p = 0.09$), coaches with 2-5 years experience (9.60 ± 2.88) scored higher than coaches with 7 years or above experience (6.00 ± 1.79) in demonstrating use of Q&A. This difference was significant ($t = 2.54$, $p = 0.032$).

Table 1.7 Percentage of time spent in coaching behaviour by Playing Experience

Behaviour Type	10 – 15 Years (%)	15 Years or Above (%)	Total (%)
Silence	4.33	10.70	8.88
Question	2.26	6.25	5.11
Model Negative	5.52	2.93	3.21
Model Positive	4.00	7.80	6.72
Hustle	3.29	3.28	3.29
Scold	1.34	3.09	2.51
Praise	22.99	17.62	19.15
Physical Assistance	5.48	5.12	5.24
Management	5.25	5.50	5.42
Post Instruction	11.99	7.73	8.95
Concurrent Instruction	21.43	18.46	19.31
Pre-Instruction	15.22	13.25	13.81
Use of Q&A	5.25	10.78	9.08
Observes	27.00	41.80	37.57

Manages	11.50	6.12	7.92
General Instruction	70.50	55.10	59.50
Use of Demonstrations	7.67	6.70	6.92

General instruction scored highest with coaches with 10 – 15 years playing experience (m = 70.50%) and coaches with 15 years or above playing experience (m = 55.10%). Concurrent instruction scored highest out of all of the instructional categories (m = 19.31%), with coaches with 10 – 15 years playing experience (m = 21.43%) and coaches with 15 years or above playing experience (m = 18.46%). Coaches with 15 years or above playing experience scored two and half times more in use of silence (m = 10.70%) than those with 10 – 15 years playing experience (m = 4.33%). Coaches with 15 years or above scored (m = 10.78%) in the use of Q&A, more than double of those coaches with 10 – 15 years playing experience (m = 5.25%). Coaches with 15 years or above playing experience (m =41.80%) scored more than one and a half times more than those with 10 – 15 years playing experience (m = 27.00%) in the observes category.

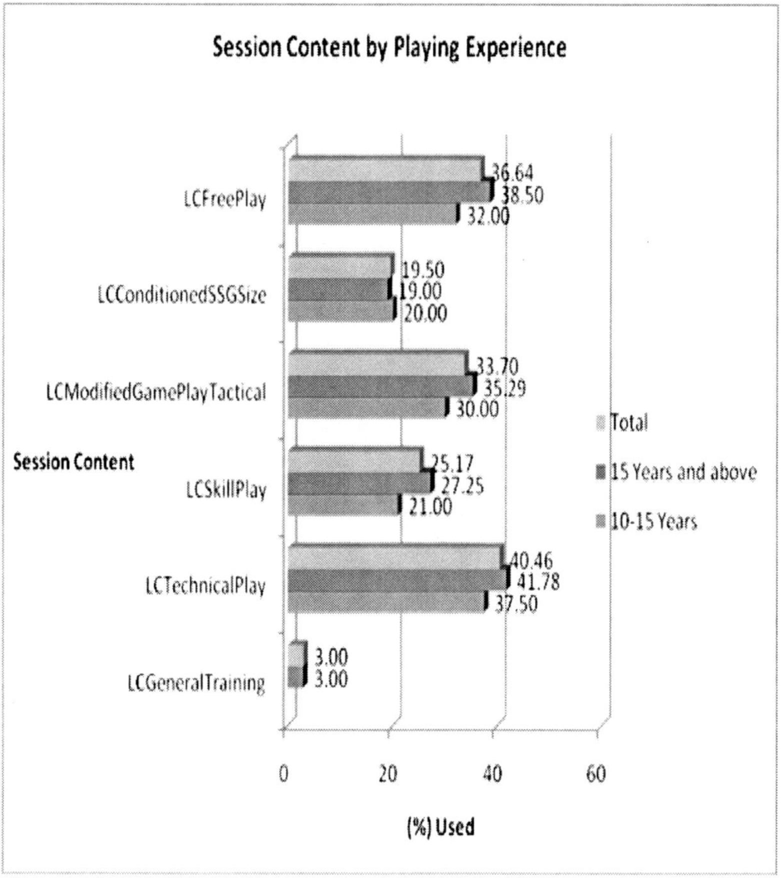

Figure 2.5 Session content by playing experience

Technical play scored highest (m = 40.46%) with conditioned SSG scoring lowest (m = 19.50%).

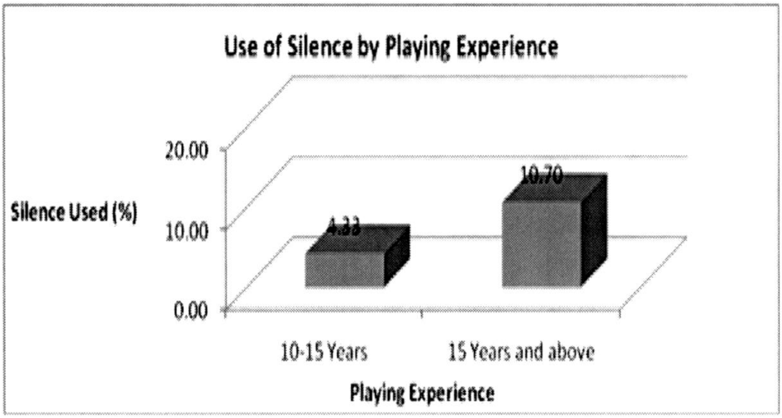

Figure 3.0 Use of silence by playing experience

The data set violated parametric assumptions of Playing Experience; (*D* (4) = 0.200, p>0.05). Therefore in order to explore relationships amongst the variables between coaches with 10 - 15 years playing experience and coaches with 15 years or above playing experience from use of silence. An Independent Samples T-test showed that coaches with 15 years or above years playing experience (mean = 10.70 ± 6.04) scored higher than coaches with 10 - 15 years or above experience (mean = 4.33 ± 0.58) in demonstrating use of silence, this difference was significant (t = -3.30, p = 0.009).

Table 1.8 Percentage of time spent in coaching behaviour by Age Group of Participants

Behaviour Type	U7's (%)	U9's (%)	U10's (%)	U12's (%)	U13's (%)	Total (%)
Silence	5.70	7.27	18.88	9.20	9.10	8.88
Question	3.82	3.69	8.20	3.45	8.97	5.11
Model Negative	2.98	4.72	3.21	1.15	0.00	3.21
Model Positive	5.71	5.10	13.17	4.60	7.39	6.72
Hustle	3.11	2.86	3.56	9.20	1.46	3.29
Scold	2.41	1.21	2.10	5.75	3.86	2.51
Praise	19.04	23.71	13.17	19.54	13.78	19.15
Physical Assistance	5.87	6.51	3.62	2.30	0.94	5.24
Management	7.35	4.03	2.83	6.90	6.91	5.42
Post Instruction	5.91	10.54	8.52	16.10	7.90	8.95
Concurrent Instruction	22.51	19.76	13.59	12.64	20.81	19.31
Pre-Instruction	14.79	12.67	12.04	8.05	19.36	13.81
Use of Q&A	7.67	7.80	17.00	7.00	7.50	9.08
Observes	29.25	33.60	49.00	60.00	41.50	37.57

Manages	5.67	8.60	6.00	10.00	13.00	7.92
General Instruction	71.75	63.80	39.50	34.00	57.00	59.50
Use of Demonstrations	8.25	6.00	8.50	7.00	4.50	6.92

Table 1.9 Percentage of time spent in specific session content by Age Group of Participants

Session Content	U7's (%)	U9's (%)	U10's (%)	U12's (%)	U13's (%)	Total (%)
LCFreeplay	30.25	29.60	36.50	37.00	67.00	36.64
LCConditionedSSG	00.00	19.50	00.00	00.00	00.00	19.50
LCModifiedGamePlayTact	30.00	31.67	33.00	42.00	47.00	33.70
LCSkillPlay	24.00	22.75	36.00	00.00	00.00	25.17
LCTechnicalPlay	48.50	35.80	41.50	26.00	44.00	40.46
LCGeneralTraining	00.00	00.00	00.00	3.00	00.00	3.00

5.0 Discussion

This chapter aims to discuss, analyse and evaluate the results from this particular study and compare, contrast and critique its findings with previous studies described in the literature review. Furthermore, through the analysis of systematic observation of youth football coaches, to aimed to determine if there were any relationships between coaches behaviour, the experience, education, football qualifications gained and the content which is being delivered in training sessions.

This study has demonstrated, with the use of the Arizona State University Observation Instrument (ASUOI) that the youth football coaches observed for the purpose of this study used similar behavioural patterns of those coaches who have been previously studied. Furthermore, by profiling each coach, analysis showed that several factors exist which can determine how a coach behaves during a practice football session. Results within this study also conflicted with some previous studies surrounding coach behaviour; however, by profiling each and every coach, a better understanding of where these discrepancies lay was achieved. The adapted version of System for Observing Fitness Instruction Time (SOFIT), namely System for Observing practice Content And coach Behaviour (SOCAB) was utilised to gain understanding of the content which was being delivered throughout the sessions. SOCAB did highlight the areas and content which was being delivered as well as highlight the areas which perhaps need to be introduced more often. By gaining this understanding of session content and coach behaviour, analytical tests were able to be performed to help achieve the research objectives (RO).

This study is in agreement to that of previous studies, Tharp and Gallimore (1976), Langsdorf (1979), Dodds and Rife (1981), and Lacy and Darst (1985), which found that the use of some sort of instruction was the most commonly used behaviour by the coaches, general instruction (m = 59.50%). Out of the three types of instruction, concurrent instruction (m = 19.31%) scored highest with post instruction (m = 8.95%) scoring the least. As these earlier studies did not illustrate nor state what kind of education the coaches had, it was important for this study to see if there were any significant differences between the FA level certification which the coaches held and the instructional behaviour which was conducted.

The coaches which held a FA Level 2 certificate scored lower in both general instruction (m = 46.25%) and concurrent instruction (m = 15.44%) than that of a FA Level 1 certificated coach (m = 64.80%) and (m = 20.85%) respectively.

However, an Independent Samples T-test showed that there were no significant differences with the use of concurrent instruction, FA Level 1Certificated Coaches (mean = 20.85 ± 6.33) against FA Level 2 Certificated Coaches (15.44 ± 4.31) (t = 1.84, p = 0.101). While this pattern of behaviour is not strongly associated with the level of certification held by the coaches, the amount of coaching experience is a key factor. An Independent Samples T-test does show that the use of general instruction by coaching experience was significantly different, coaches with two – five years coaching experience (mean = 65.50 ± 10.15) against coaches with five – seven years experience (mean = 39.50 ± 2.12) (t = 5.90, p = 0.14).

However, although this research study has underpinned what previous studies have found, Tharp and Gallimore (1976), Langsdorf (1979), Dodds and Rife (1981), and Lacy and Darst (1985), in that instruction remains the most used behaviour by a coach, the results do not allow for instruction interpretation. For example, if youth football coaches are instructing the participants for more than half of the session, one could argue that this instruction had a positive effect or, indeed, negative. Furthermore, because concurrent instruction was the highest single form of instructional behaviour, further analysis would have to be performed to investigate which behaviour, if any, was being used during this time. Perhaps because the participants were young people, one could assume that the coach was praising the children to encourage their learning. However, a Pearson correlation test was performed and showed that there was no positive correlation between concurrent instruction and the use of praise ($r = 7.73$, $n = 14$, $p > .0005$). In Smith *et al's* (2006) study a coach talks about the impact instruction can have on children when delivering a training session, the coach explains, 'give instruction but not overwhelm the kids with instruction, you can't take everything in all at once'. Therefore, if concurrent instruction was the one single, most used behaviour during this study and praise did not correlate with this finding then further research would be needed to establish exactly what was being said during the concurrent instructional time.

Although the coaches in this study showed a high level of instruction and could well have impacted positively, there is still that risk that they were overloading the participants with information and therefore had a negative impact on the participants learning. However, due to the limitations of this study and, more specifically, the instrumentation used, it is impossible to know exactly what information was being relayed from coach to athlete during this instruction time. Therefore, further testing and observational methods would be necessary to establish exactly what was being said during this time. More *et al* (1996) used the Coach Analysis Instrument (CAI) which is an instrument used to systematically examine the effectiveness of verbal coaching behaviour and to record verbal content from a coach. By introducing this additional system, a more accurate data could be recorded. Gould, *et al* (1990), Salmela (1996), Cushion (2001), Gilbert and Trudel (2001), and Cushion *et al* (2003: pp. 215) all state that it is experience and the observation of other coaches that remain the primary sources of knowledge for coaches, and that coach education and continuing professional development fail to draw effectively on this experience. When referring to the coaches' behaviour in this study, early analysis augments these authors theory. For example, the coaches who have the most coaching experience appear to be using less instruction thus using the behavioural action of silence which allows for a more analytical approach.

Although it is recognised that instruction is an important aspect to coaching, and that effective coaching instruction is an essential component, a proficient coach however, needs a variety of pedagogical skills Schmidt (1988) and Lee *et al* (1993). Referring back to Smith *et al's* (2006) study, where a coach, when interviewed, explains that silence was necessary by the coaches to observe and analyse, it would suggest that the more experienced coaches and the coaches with a higher level of certificate involved during this research were indeed using silence more to assist with their analytical approach due to the fact that they were instructing less. Independent T-tests identified that coaches with a FA Level 2 certificate (mean = 15.43 ± 4.91) do in fact use silence more than those with a FA Level 1 certificate (6.26 ± 3.84) and could therefore be argued that the education gained through certification can be a factor in how a coach uses the silence behaviour. However, when testing the use of silence by coaching experience it was coaches with five – seven years coaching experience (mean =

18.88 ± 0.98) which scored higher than Coaches with seven years or above experience (mean = 6.63 ± 4.36) which therefore contradicts Gould *et al* (1990), Salmela (1996), Cushion (2001), Gilbert and Trudel (2001), and Cushion *et al* (2003) statement about experience, especially if successful elite professional youth football coaches are saying it is paramount to use silence to observe as explained in Smith *et al's* (2006) study. Perhaps then, the coaches who have more coaching experience are the coaches who have failed to draw upon the education available to them by acquiring a FA Level 2 certificate and therefore have not been educated in the importance of silence. Perhaps the coaches with more coaching experience are older in age and are drawing upon their own experiences where instruction was the key to their own successes.

This would certainly reflect to what Abraham and Collins (1998) theorise when insisting that coaches' knowledge and action can be viewed as both the product and manifestation of a personally experienced involvement with the coaching process and that they are linked to the coaches' own histories and, crucially, are attributable to how they were learned

The real reasons behind such findings and the reasons why the use of silence differs between coaches with various experiences and qualifications would be best interpreted by the coaches themselves and further qualitative research would be needed. In Smith *et al's* (2006) study it was stated that the use of silence is important within the coaching environment as this time can be used to observe and analyse. One could assume that this is a reasonable concept and that, indeed, the coaches during this study used silence for exactly that purpose. However, a Pearson correlation test was conducted and showed that there was no correlation between the use of silence and observing ($r = 39.94$, $n = 14$, $p < .0005$). Therefore, if the coaches were not observing the participants during the time they were being silent, it does raise questions over what exactly the coach was doing during this time and if the coach utilised this important time effectively. Indeed, during a specific observation, it was evident that the coach was performing the behaviour of silence, however, he was not engaged in the observation of the participants instead he was seen to be off task and actually talking to the parents. Certainly one could argue that the coach was engaging in personal relations with the parents, however, within the coaching context, it could be argued that this is poor coaching practice and that the use of silence should indeed be utilised for observing and analysing the session.

Jones *et al* (1998) insist that if coach education programs continue to focus on content then they will run the risk of simply having a modernised version of the same. This statement certainly holds some strength in its argument. For example, within this study it has suggested that coaches are not utilising their behaviours in the most positive way meaning that instead of observing the session and participants during the use of silence, it appears that the coach was simply off task and not interacting positively thus focussing more on the delivery of the content. Furthermore, during the use of concurrent instruction, it is impossible to state from this study what instruction was being issued to the participants but it does state that praise was not being used during this time thus not utilising the concurrent instruction positively. Jones (2000) argues that coach education courses, having been developed along rationalistic lines, currently do not develop intellectual, and practical competencies, namely, independent and creative thinking skills in relation to meaning making and problem solving. Macdonald and Tinning (1995) and Potrac *et al* (2000) also agree and state that by separating theory from practice in educational courses, high level tasks have been presented as sequential routine, which has resulted in the deskilling of the practitioner in terms of cognitive and human interaction.

If youth coaches are simply delivering content which has been passed on to them by coach education courses then it could be argued that youth football coaching has become a non-challenging environment for its participants. Certainly within this study it would appear that there is a case for and against this statement. For example, use of Q&A could have served as a good tool to pose problems to the participants as well as challenge their existing knowledge and ensuring that they understood what the coach was delivering. However, the use of Q&A was only the seventh most used behaviour during this study.

Furthermore, Independent Samples T-tests showed that coaches with five-seven years of experience (mean = 17.00 ± 1.41) scored higher than coaches with seven years or above coaching experience (6.00 ± 1.79), this difference was significant (8.88, p = 0.09), coaches with two-five years experience (9.60 ± 2.88) also scored higher than coaches with seven years or above experience (6.00 ±

1.79) in demonstrating use of Q&A, this difference was significant ($t = 2.54$, $p = 0.032$). However, when testing coaches with the varying levels of FA certificates gained, an Independent Samples T-test showed that FA Level 2 Certificated Coaches (mean = 14.75 ± 2.97) scored higher than FA Level 1 Certificated Coaches (6.56 ± 1.67) in demonstrating use of Q&A, this difference was significant ($t = -6.463$, $p = 0.007$). Therefore, it could be argued that coaching qualifications and the content of these courses are in fact educating the coaches to be more challenging. However, this study and the limitations of the instruments used, it cannot be established if the use of Q&A was purposefully used to challenge the participants.

6.0 Conclusion & Recommendations

Through the analysis of systematic observation of youth football coaches, this study aimed to explore if there were any relationships between the football qualifications gained from a football coach and how a coach behaves and interacts with the participants during delivery of a coaching session. Furthermore, it aimed to identify if there were any relationships between the ways various coaches behave, the experience and education which the coaches have received and, the content delivered. Whilst recognising the limitations of this study design, perhaps the most significant finding was the use of instruction within a coaching session and more specifically the use of concurrent instruction. Whilst an understanding has been gained through this study about the importance of instruction and how it can play an important role within the coaching process, the study has also found that too much instruction can hinder a participants learning environment thus having a negative impact on its participants. With concurrent instruction being the highest single behaviour used within this study, one could argue that concerns are raised as to what instruction was issued especially if praise was not a prominent behaviour during this time. However, due to the limitations of this study and, more specifically, the instrumentation used, it is impossible to know exactly what information was being relayed from coach to athlete during this instruction time. Therefore, further testing and observational methods would be necessary to establish exactly what was being said during this time. More *et al* (1996) used the Coach Analysis Instrument (CAI) which is an instrument used to systematically examine the effectiveness of verbal coaching behaviour and to record verbal content from a coach. By introducing this additional system, a more accurate data could be recorded. Furthermore, by attaching Dictaphones to each coach, future studies of this nature will be able to listen to exactly what instruction was being relayed.

Within this study it was coaches with more years experience which drew effectively on the need to instruct less which augmented Gould, *et al* (1990), Salmela (1996), Cushion (2001), Gilbert and Trudel (2001), and Cushion *et al* (2003: pp. 215) statement insisting that it is experience and the observation of other coaches that remain the primary sources of knowledge for coaches. The coaches who had the most coaching experience appeared to have been using less instruction thus using the behavioural action of silence which allows for a more analytical approach. However, it was the coach with a higher level of coaching certificate which used the silence behaviour most as opposed to those coaches with more experience. Although silence scored a high amount of behaviour time, it was evident in this study that the coaches did not use this time effectively. Indeed, some observations saw that coaches were off task, and more specifically, not involved in the session whatsoever but instead was engaged in talking to parents on the sideline. It could be argued that this was not good coaching practice and that the coaches and participants alike would benefit hugely if the coaches utilised the silence time to actually observe and analyse.

Macdonald and Tinning (1995), Jones *et al* (1998) and Potrac *et al* (2000) insist that if coach education programs continue to focus on content then they will run the risk of simply having a modernised version of the same. Furthermore, coach education courses, having been developed along rationalistic lines, currently do not develop intellectual, and practical competencies, namely, independent and creative thinking skills in relation to meaning making and problem solving; this has resulted in the deskilling of the practitioner in terms of cognitive and human interaction. However, once again, it was coaches with less experience and higher level of certification which scored highest in this category. During this study it was evident that the use of Q&A was completely underused and thus can be argued was completely under valued by the coaches. For example, use of Q&A could have served as a good tool to pose problems to the participants as well as challenge their existing knowledge and ensuring that they understood what the coach was delivering. Therefore, it could be argued that youth football coaching has become a non-challenging environment for its participants. If this is true with the wider population, and further research would be needed to prove this, then it can be argued that young football players are not receiving the best possible coaching from the nation's coaches.

The use of SOCAB (System for Observing Coaching content And Behaviour) was able to illustrate what content was being delivered during the practice sessions. This information was useful as it highlights which areas of coaching are being delivered throughout youth football. However, due to the limitations of SOCAB, this study was unable to distinguish between what was being delivered, when it was delivered during the session and how it was delivered. For example, although it would appear that each content topic was being covered by the coach it does not indicate if the content was being delivered in a structured, progressive fashion. Furthermore, it does not highlight the style in which the content was delivered either and therefore, SOCAB would need to be used in conjunction with other instrumentation for it to be critically analytical. However, when used along side the ASUOI and for the purpose of this study, the information which SOCAB produced was exceptionally useful. If SOCAB was to be introduced to the analysis of systematic observations, it would need to be tested more vigorously with a wider population to enable it to be validated.

Through the analysis of systematic observation of youth football coaches, the purpose of this study was to determine if there were any relationships between coaches behaviour, the experience, education, football qualifications gained and the content which is being delivered in training sessions. The evidence within this study certainly suggests that the level of qualification held by a coaching practitioner is a key factor in how a coach behaves and that this behaviour follows good coaching practice. However, it was coaches with more coaching experience which failed draw upon this experience to illustrate effective coaching practice. Whilst coaching experience and level of qualification held by the practitioner can be argued to be major factors in how a coach behaves during a practice session, this study is in agreement Cross and Lyle (2004) claim that the coaching process is a complex and messy subject and that there are many factors which can determine how a coach behaves.

This study has not only augmented previous studies and theories, it has also contradicted them. It indicates just how complex coaching behaviour can be when viewing it in a sociological context surrounding the coaching process. Whilst this study has highlighted the common behaviours used by youth football coaches during a practice session and illustrated what factors may have affected these behaviours, there are still many areas within the coaching environment and the coaching process which need to be explored in more depth. However, it is hoped that this study can be used as a foundation on which to build upon in respect to future studies surrounding youth football coaching ensuring that an even more critical understanding of coach behaviour, coach education and the coaching process can be achieved.

Reference List

Abraham, A., and Collins, D. (1998), 'Examining and Extending Research in Coach Development', *Quest*, 1, (50), pp. 59 - 79.

Brewer, C. J. and Jones, R. L. (2002), 'A Five-stage Process For Establishing Contextually Valid Systematic Observation Instruments: The Case Of Rugby Union', *The Sports Psychologist*, 16, (1), pp. 138 – 159.

Cote, J., Salmela, J. H., and Russell, S. (1995), 'The Knowledge Of High Performance Gymnastics Coaches: Competition And Training Considerations', *The Sport Psychologist*, 9, (1), pp. 76 – 95.

Claxton, D. B. (1988), 'A Systematic Observation Of More Or Less Successful High School Tennis Coaches', *Journal Of Teaching In Physical Education*, 7, pp. 302 – 310.

Cushion, C. J., Armour, K. M., and Jones, R. L. (2006), 'Locating The Coaching Process In Practice: Models 'For' And 'Of' Coaching', *Physical Education and Sport Pedagogy*, 11, (1), pp. 83-89.

Cushion, C. J., Armour, K. M., and Jones, R. L. (2003), 'Coach Education and Continuing Professional Development: Experience and Learning to Coach', *National Association for Physical Education in Higher Education*, 55, (1), pp. 215-230.

Cross, N. and Lyle, J. (2000), *The Coaching Process: Principles and Practice For Sport*, Oxford: Reed Educational and Professional Publishing Limited.

DeMarco, G. M. P., Mancini, V. H., Wuest, D. A., and Schempp, P. (1996), 'Becoming Reacquainted With A Once Familiar And Still Valuable Tool: Systematic Observation Methodology Revisited', *International Journal of Physical Education*, 32, (1), pp. 17 – 26.

Dodds, P., and Rife, F. (1981), cited in Miller, A. W. (1992), 'Systematic Observation Behaviour Similarities Of Youth Sport Soccer Coaches', *Physical Educator*, 49, (3), pp. 1.

Gallimore, R., and Tharpe, R. (2004), 'What A Coach Can Teach A Teacher, 1975–2004: Reflections And Reanalysis Of John Wooden's Teaching Practices', *The Sport Psychologist*, 18, pp. 119 – 137.

Gilbert, W., Cote, J., and mallet, C. (2006), 'Developmental Paths and Activities of Successful Sport Coaches', *International Journal of Sports Science and Coaching*, 1, (1), pp. 69 – 76.

Gilbert, W., and Trudel, P. (2001), 'Learning To Coach Through Experience: Reflection In Model Youth Sport Coaches', *Journal Of Teaching In Physical Education*, 21, (1), pp. 16 – 34.

Gould, D., Gianinni, J., Krane, J., and Hodge, K. (1990), 'Educational Needs of Elite U.S. National Pan American and Olympic Coaches', *Journal of Teaching in Physical Education*, 1, (9), pp. 322-344.

Gratton, C., and Jones, I. (2004), *Research Methods For Sport Studies*, London: Routledge.

Holborn, M., and Langley, P. (2004), *Sociology Themes And Perspectives*, London: HarperCollins Publishers Limited.

Jones, R. L. (2000), Toward a Sociology of Coaching cited in Jones, R. L., and Armour, K. M. (2000), *The Sociology of Sport: Theory and Practice*, London: Longman.

Jones, R. L., Armour, K. M., and Potrac, P. (1998), *The Cultures of Coaching*, London: Longman.

Kahan, D. (1999), 'Coaching Behaviour: A Review Of The Systematic Observation Research Literature', *Applied Research in Coaching and Athletics Annual*, 14, (1), pp. 17 – 58.

Lacy, A.C., and Darst, P.D. (1984), 'The Evolution Of A Systematic Observation Instrument', *Journal Of Teaching In Physical Education*, 3, pp. 59 - 66.

Lacy, A.C., and Darst, P.D. (1985), 'Systematic Observation Of Behaviours Of Winning High School Head Football Coaches', *Journal Of Teaching In Physical Education*, 4, pp. 256 - 270.

Lacy, A. C. (1989), cited in Miller, A. W. (1992), 'Systematic Observation Behaviour Similarities Of Youth Sport Soccer Coaches', *Physical Educator*, 49, (3).

Lacy, A.C., and Martin, D.M. (1994), 'Analysis of Starter/Nonstarter Motor-Skill Engagement and Coaching

Behaviours in Collegiate Women's Volleyball', *Journal Of Teaching In Physical Education*, 13, (1), pp. 95.

Langsdorf, E. V. (1979) cited in Miller, A. W. (1992), 'Systematic Observation Behaviour Similarities Of Youth Sport Soccer Coaches', *Physical Educator*, 49, (3), pp. 1.

Lee, A. C., Keh, N. C., and Magill, R. A. (1993), 'Instructional Effects Of Teacher Feedback In Physical Education', *Journal Of Teaching Physical Education*, 16, (1), pp. 228 – 243.

Macdonald, D., and Tinning, R. (1995), 'Physical Education Teacher Education and The Trend to Proletarianisation: A Case Study', *Journal of Teaching in Physical Education*, 15, (1), pp. 98 – 118.

McKenzie, T.L., Sallis, J.F., and Nadar, P.R. (1991), 'SOFIT: System for Observing Fitness Instruction Time', *Journal Of Teaching In Physical Education*, 11, (1), pp. 196.

McKenzie, T.L., Stone, E.J., Feldman, H.A., Epping, J.N., Yang, M., Strikmiller, P.K., Lytle, L.A., and Parcel, G.S. (2001), 'Effects of the CATCH Physical Education Intervention Teacher Type and Lesson Location', *American Journal Of Preventative Medicine*, 21, (2), pp. 101.

Miller, A. W. (1992), 'Systematic Observation Behaviour Similarities Of Youth Sport Soccer Coaches', *Physical Educator*, 49, (3).

More, K. G., McGarry, T., Partridge, D., and Franks, I. M. (1996), 'A Computer-Assisted Analysis of Verbal Coaching Behaviour In Soccer', *Journal Of Sport Behaviour*, 19, (4), pp. 319 – 337.

Pallant,, J. (2005), *SPSS Survival Manual*, Berkshire: Open University Press.

Potrac, P., and Jones, R.L. (1999), 'The Invisible Ingredient in Coaching Knowledge: A Case For Recognising and Researching The Social Component', *Sociology Of Sport*, 2, (1), pp. 52.

Potrac, P., Jones, R., and Armour, K. (2002), 'It's All About Getting Respect: The Coaching Behaviours Of An Expert English Soccer Coach', *Sport, Education and Society*, 7, (2), pp. 183.

Potrac, P., Jones, R. L., Brewer, C., Armour, K., and Hoff, J. (2000), 'Toward an Holistic Understanding of the Coaching Process', *Quest*, 52, pp. 186 – 199.

Potrac, P., Jones, R., and Cushion, C. (2007), 'Understanding Power And The Coach's Role In Professional English Soccer: A Preliminary Investigation Of Coach Behaviour', *Soccer and Society*, 8, (1), pp. 36.

Rodgers, W., Reade, I., and Hall, C. (2007), 'Factors That Influence Coaches' Use Of Sound Coaching Practice', *International Journal of Sports Science and Coaching*, 2, (2), pp. 156.

Rowe, P.J., Schuldheisz, J.M., and van der Mars, H. (1997), 'Validation of SOFIT for Measuring Physical Activity of First to Eighth Grade Students', *Pediatric Exercise Science*, 9, (1), pp. 136.

Rupert, T. and Buschner, C. (1989), 'Teaching And Coaching: A Comparison Of Instructional Behaviours', *Journal Of Teaching In Physical Education*, 9, (1), pp. 49 – 57.

Salmela, J. H. (1996), *Great Job Coach: Getting The Edge From Proven Winners*, Ottawa, Canada: Potentium, The Coaching Network.

Salmela, J. H., Cote, J., and Baria, A. (1994), 'The Structure of Expert Knowledge in Coaches', *Advances in Sport Psychology*, 1, (2), pp. 56-65.

Schmidt, R. A. (1988), *Motor Control And Learning: A Behavioural Emphasis*, Champaign: Human Kinetics.

Smith, M., and Cushion, C. J. (2006), 'An Investigation Of The In-Game Behaviours Of Professional, Top-Level Youth Soccer Coaches', *Journal of Sports Science*, 24, (4), pp. 355 - 366.

Smith, Smoll, and Hunt (1978) cited in Smoll, F. L. and Smith, R. E. (2006), 'Leadership Behaviours in Sport: A Theoretical Model and Research Paradigm', *Journal of Applied Social Psychology*, 19, (18).

Tenenbaum, G. and Driscoll, M. P. (2005), *Methods Of Research In Sports Science*, Oxford: Meyer and Meyer Sport (UK) Limited.

Tharp, R. G., and Gallimore, R. (1976), 'What A Coach Can Teach A Teacher', *Psychology Today*, 9, (1), pp. 75 – 78.

Thomas, J. R., Nelson, J. K., and Silverman, S. J. (2005), *Research Methods In Physical Activity*, Leeds: Human Kinetics.

Trudel, P., Cote, J., and Donohue, J. (1993), 'Direct Observations Of Coaches' Behaviours During Training And Competition: A Literature Review', cited in S. Serpa, J. Alves, V. Ferreira, and A. Paulo-Brito (Eds.), *Proceedings Of The VIII World Congress of Sport Psychology,* (pp. 316 – 319).

Werthner, P., and Trudel, P. A. (2006), 'A New Theoretical Perspective for Understanding How Coaches Learn to Coach', The Sport Psychologist, 20, (1), pp. 196 – 212.

Brooking, T. Sir. (2006), 'Online Learning Here', [online], (22nd February 2006), http://www.thefa.com/TheFA/FALearning/NewsAndFeatures/Postings/2006/02/Trevor_brooking_computers_launch.htm, accessed: 1st October 2008.

Upson, M. (2006), 'Online Learning Here', [online], (22nd February 2006), http://www.thefa.com/TheFA/FALearning/NewsAndFeatures/Postings/2006/02/Trevor_brooking_computers_launch.htm, accessed: 1st October 2008.

Lightning Source UK Ltd.
Milton Keynes UK
UKOW02f2159120417
298983UK00005B/392/P

9 781326 490638